AF266694

BEAUTIFUL OUT OF THE WAY PLACES IN BEAUTIFUL WYOMING: THROUGH TERRI'S EYES.

I am really proud of this book and I want to share with you places that are my favorite places to visit in this state. My family and I and our little dog , live in Wyoming and just love it. As you journey through this book, I hope you will enjoy some of our state's beautiful landscapes, wildlife and scenery that is offered here. I really enjoyed making this book and showing what this state has to offer.

I will introduce myself, my name is Terri Strickland-Odell and I am an only child. I have a Master's Degree in Social Work. I grew up in a Episcopal church family. My father is an Episcopal priest and now a Bishop. With his position we moved around and had the greatest advantage to seeing God's country. My mother is a Registered Nurse and with that, her profession has allowed her to be employed anywhere. Growing up, my family and I had a real love for the outdoors. We loved being outdoors, and being out in Nature. I have always had a fascination with photography and seeing the world through a lens. My husband and I and our little dog find opportunity's to go and capture different things on camera. So, I hope as you see these photo's you will enjoy and see some of God's beautiful and wonderful creations.

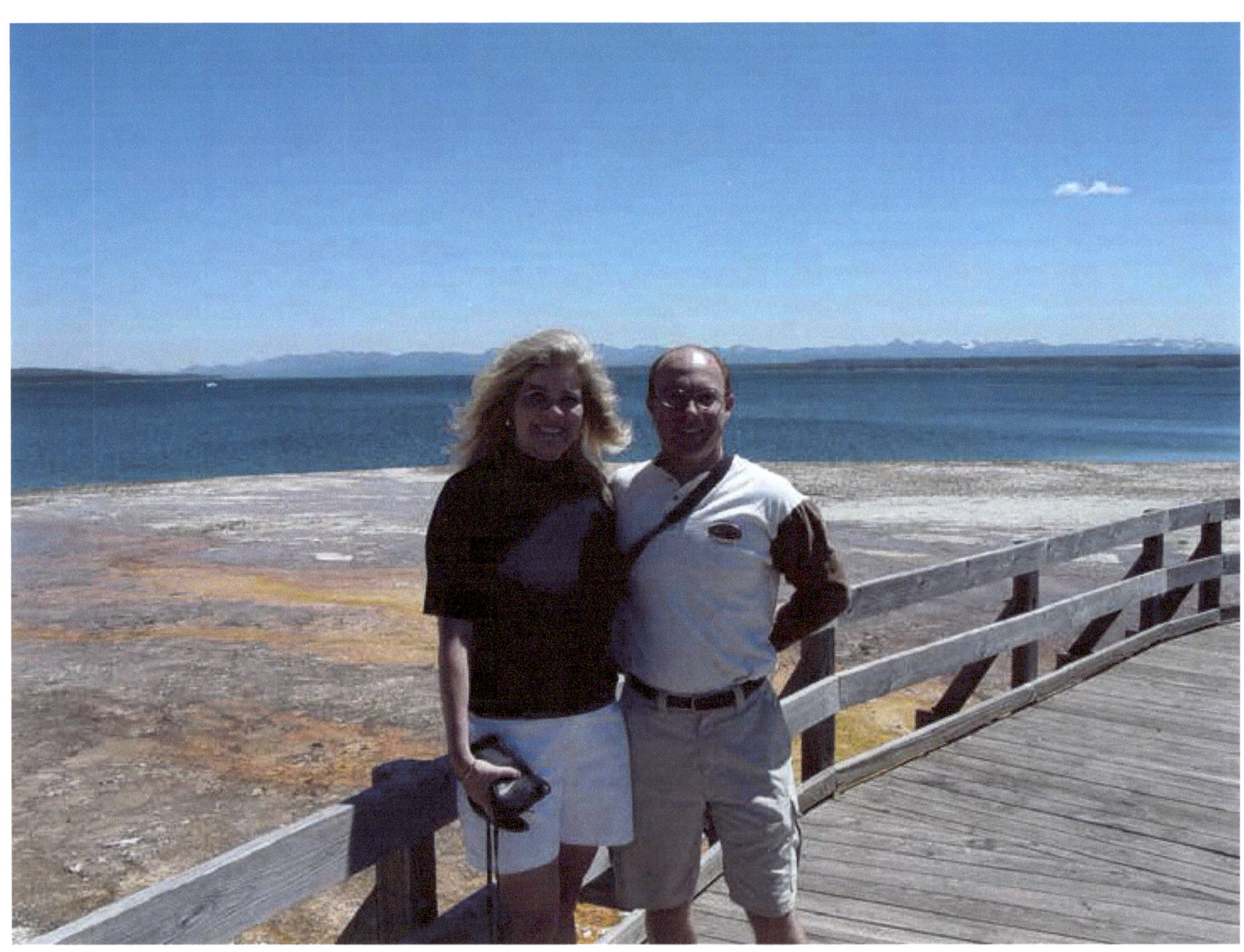

My husband and I on our Honeymoon in Yellowstone National Park.

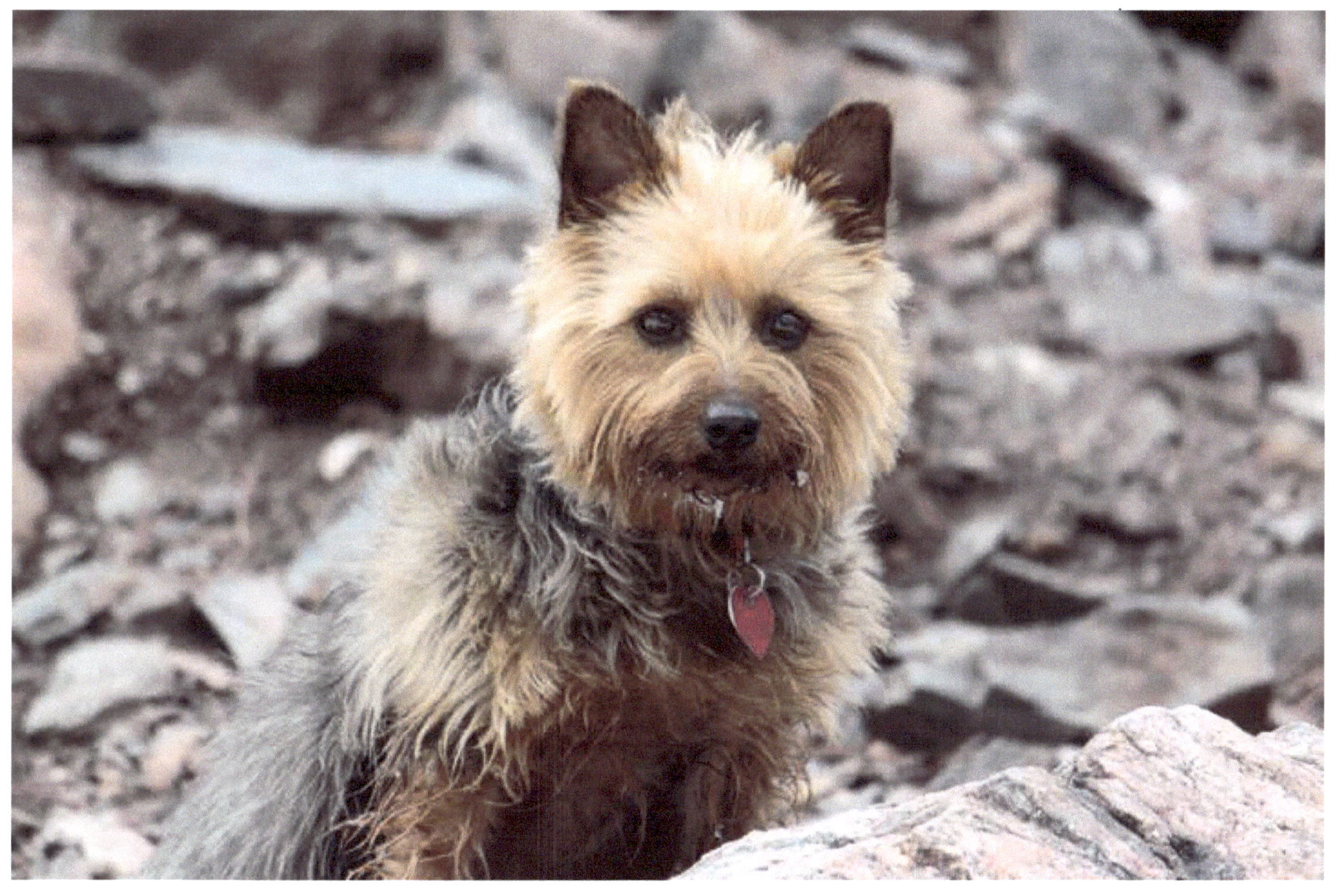

Our precious dog, Pepper sitting on the rocks.

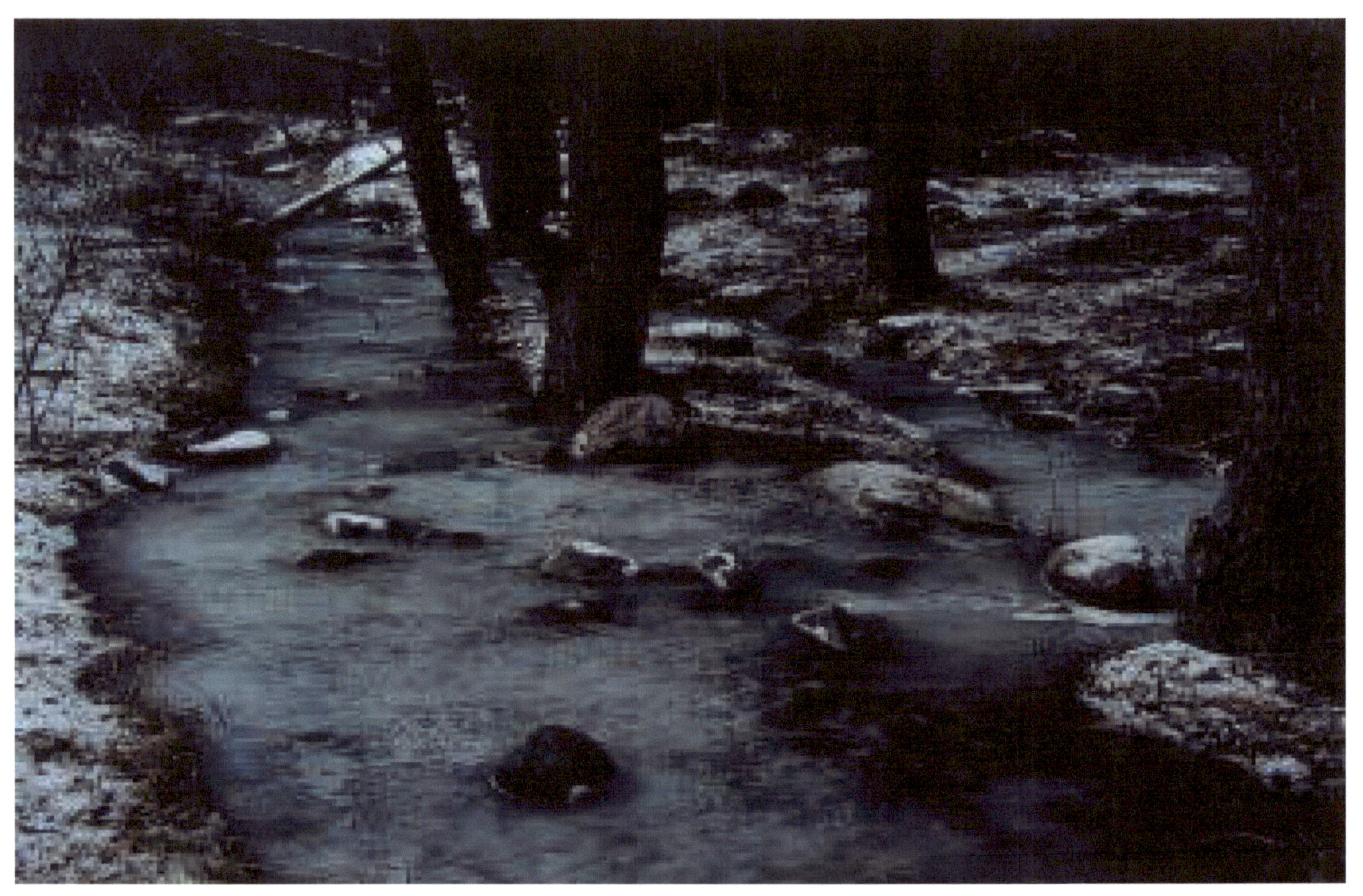

Winter time in the northern part of the Rockies in Wyoming. This was a place off the beaten path and I loved the rocks frozen in the creek bed.

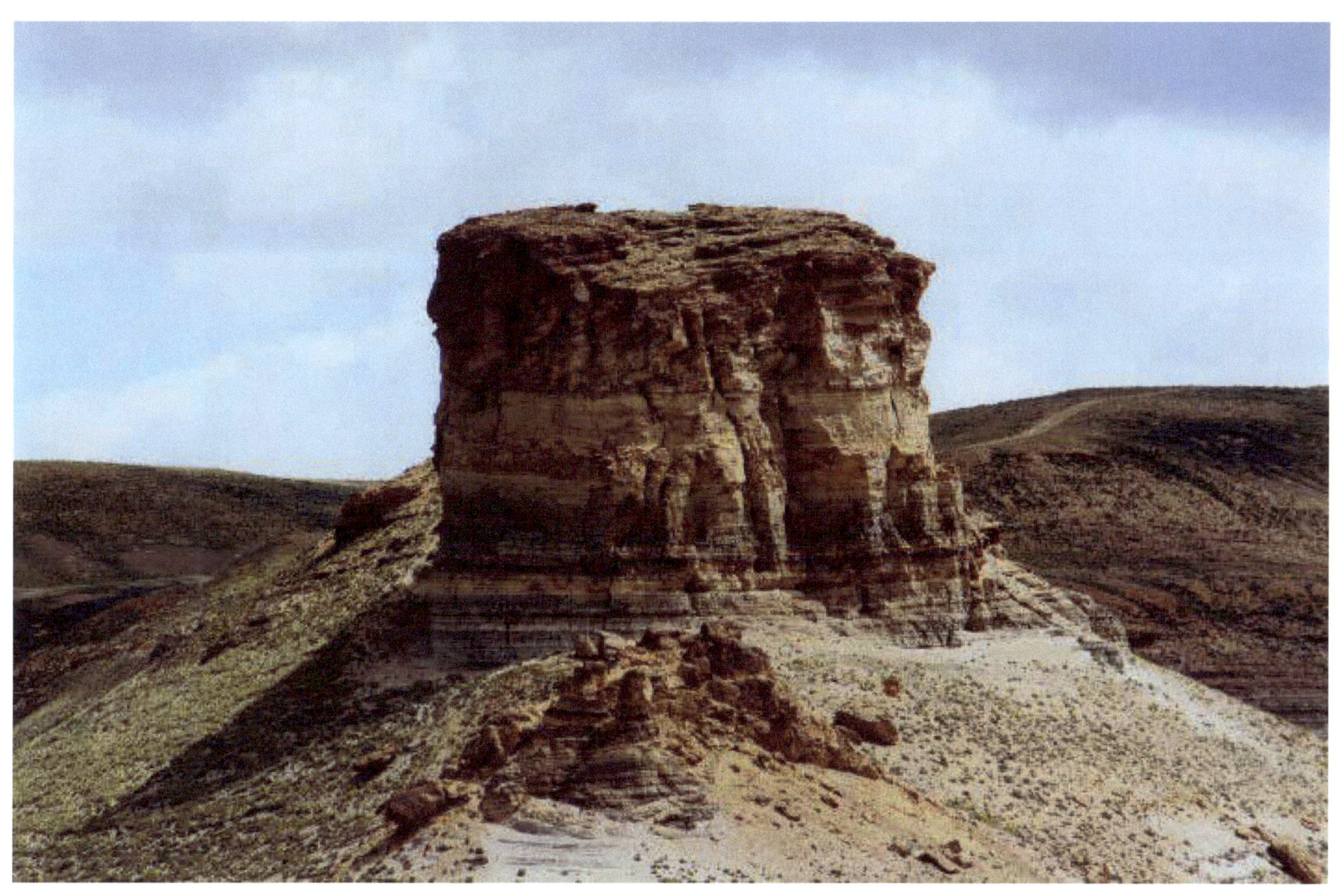

This was right off the path in Southwest Wyoming. This is Castle Rock, Green River, Wyoming.

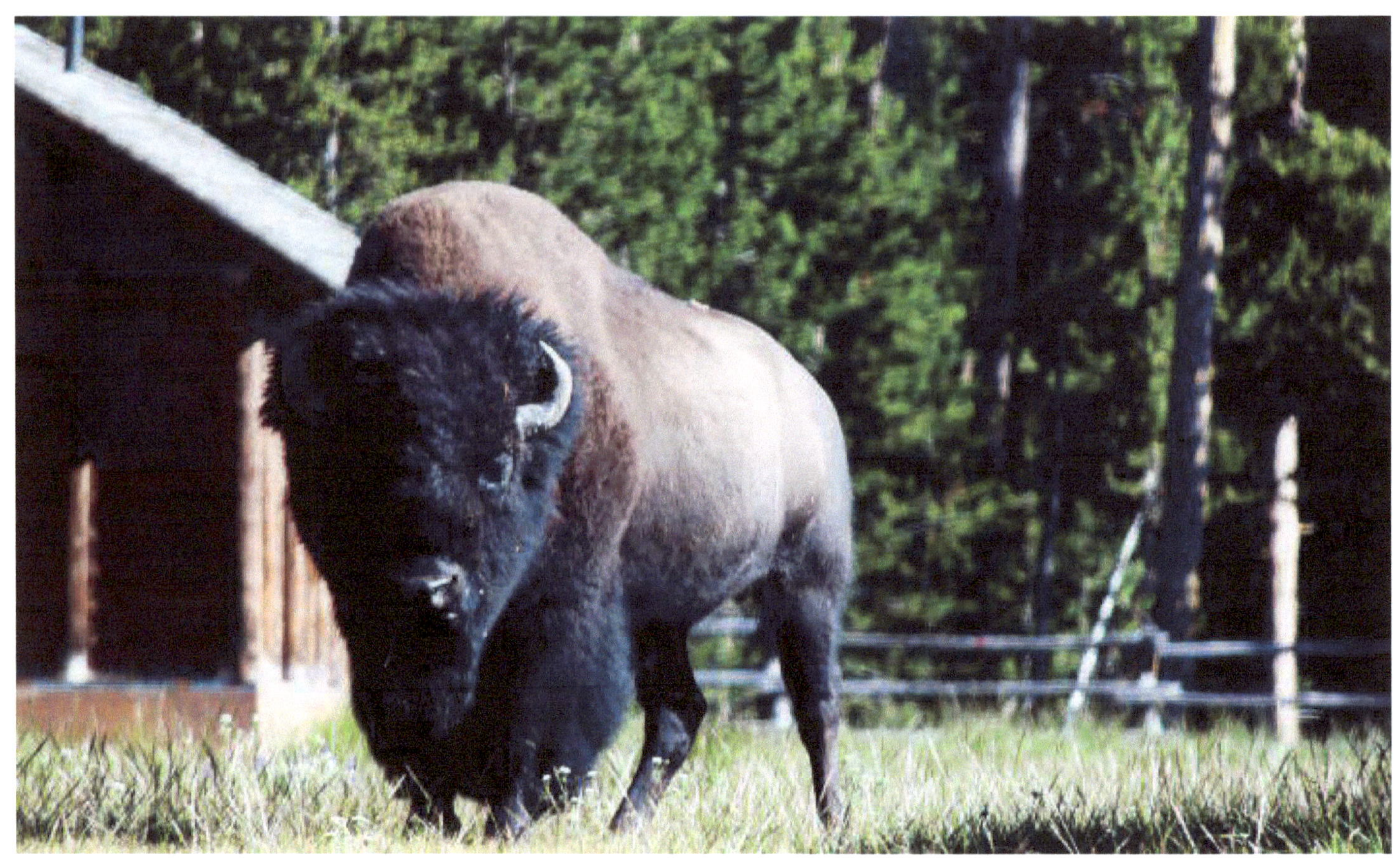

A lurking Buffalo in Yellowstone!

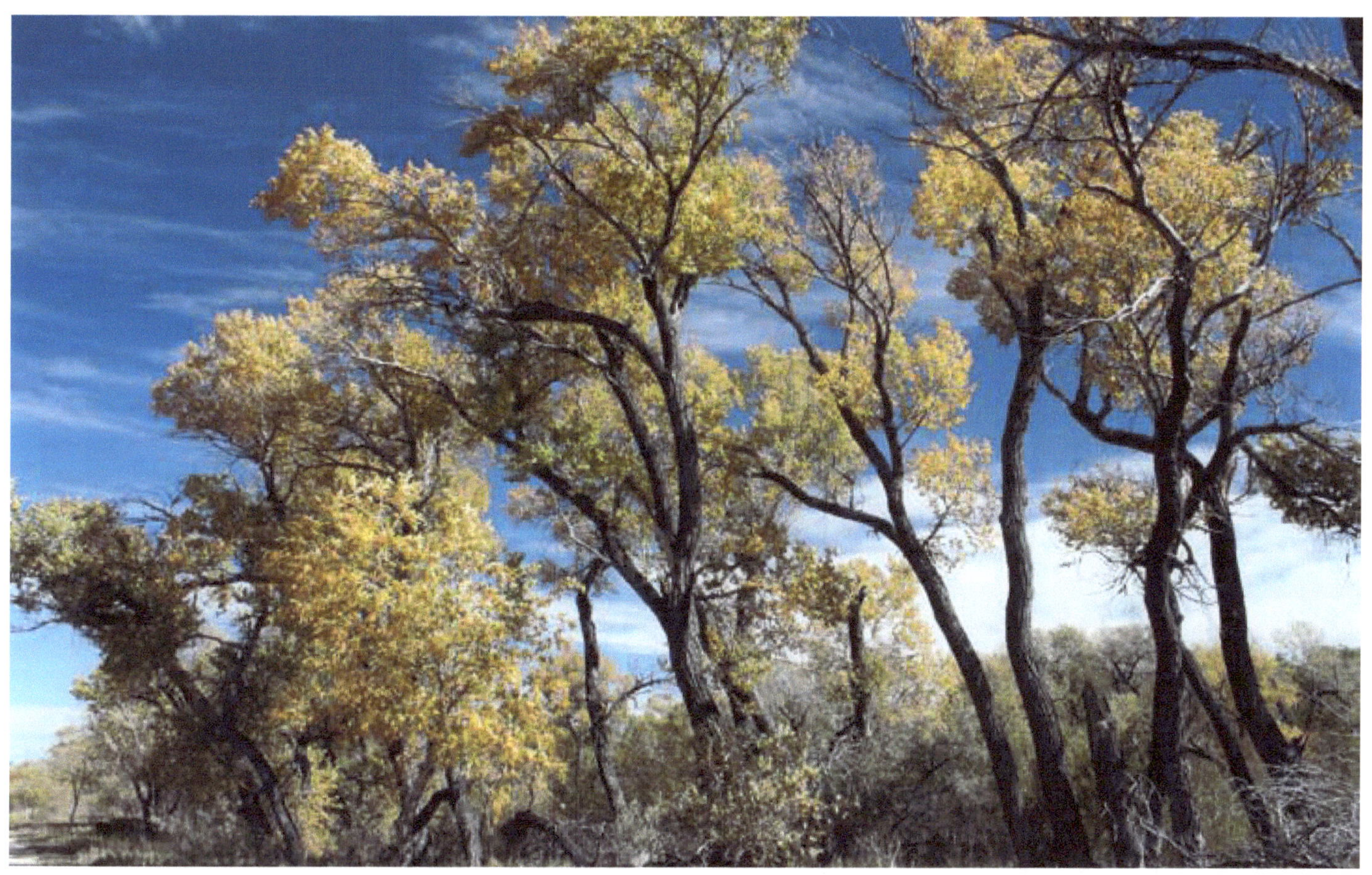

One of my favorite shots that I took this year. I love the blue sky with the white clouds in the background. This is in Northern part of the state, this fall in 2010.

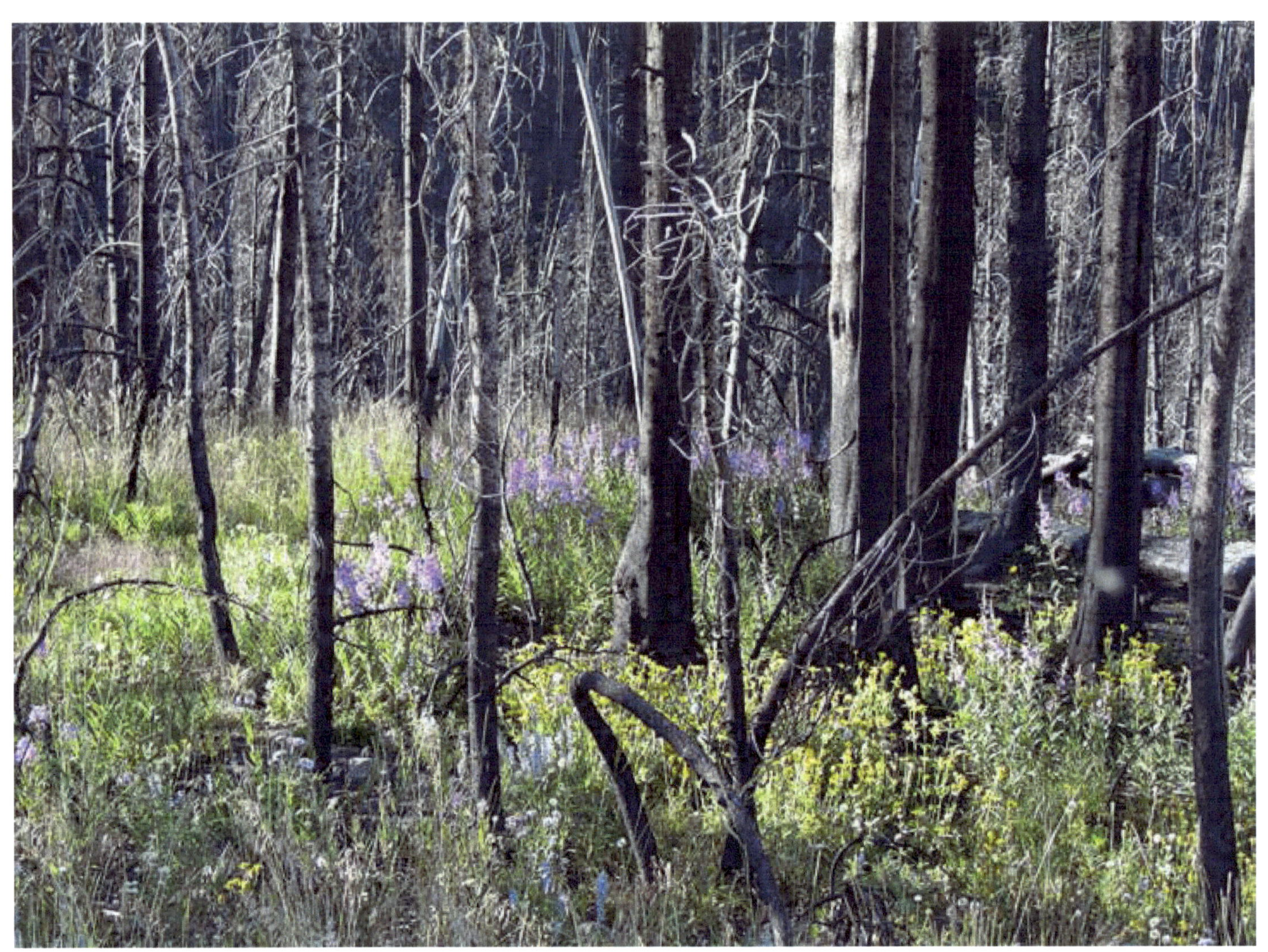

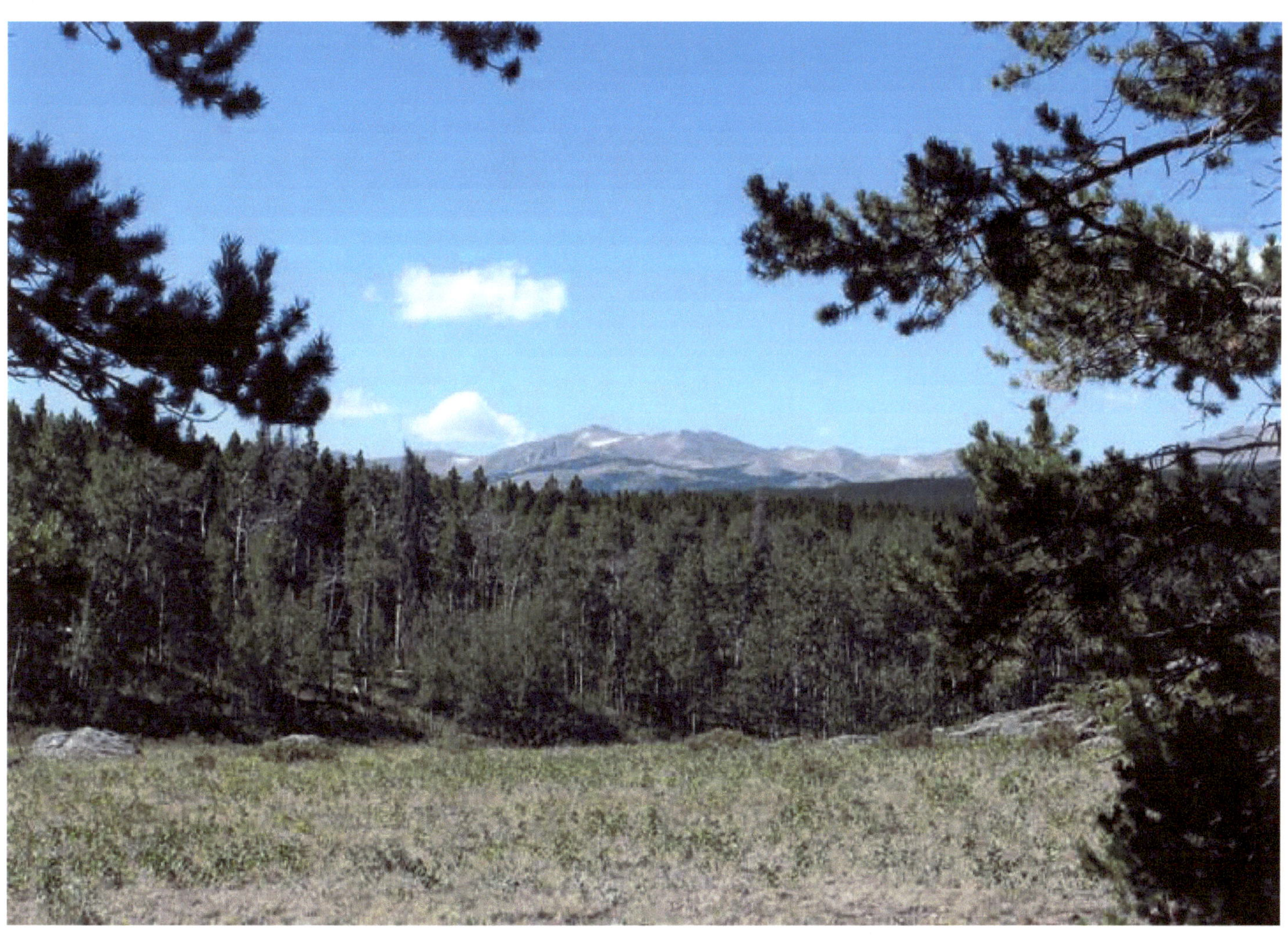

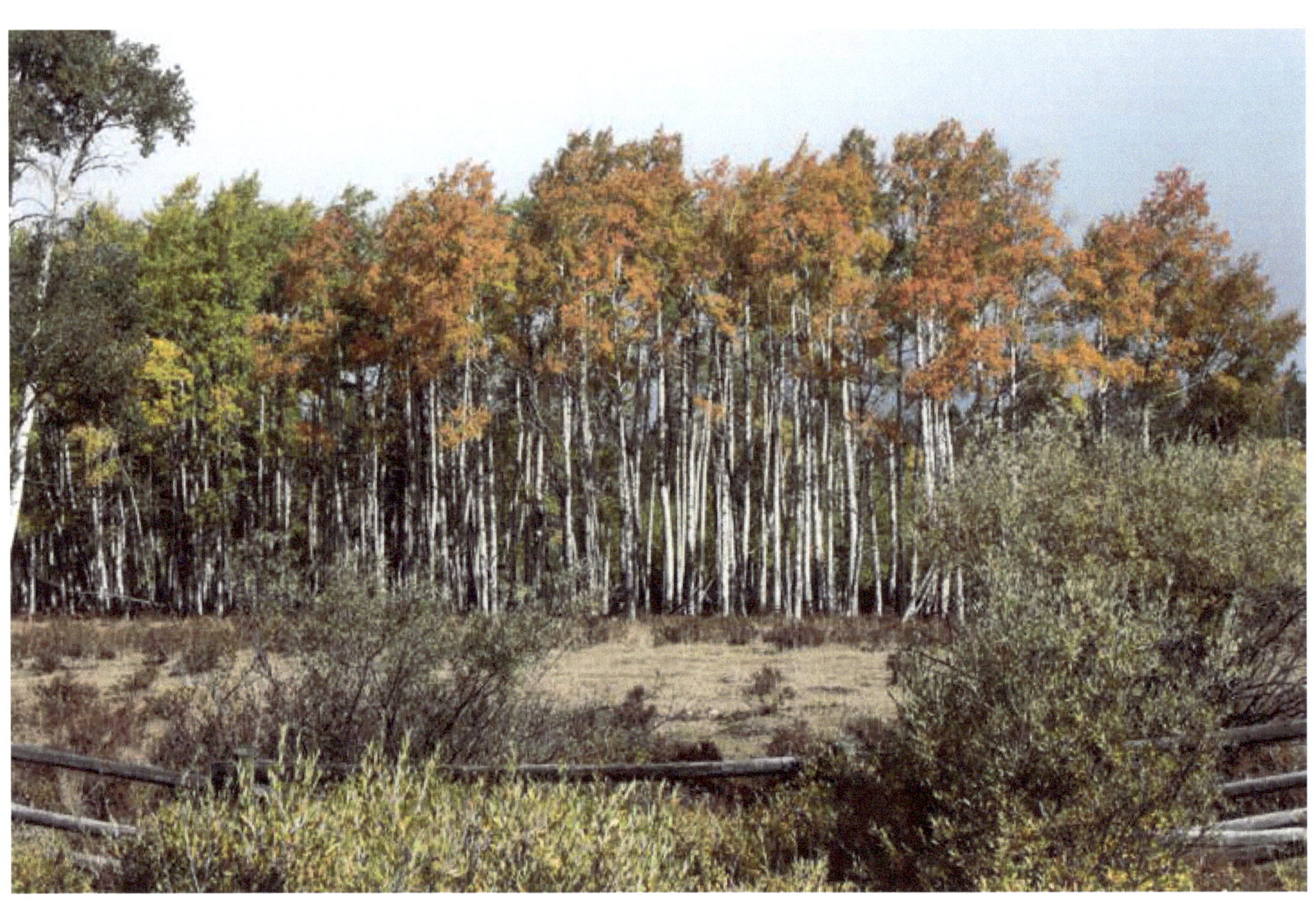

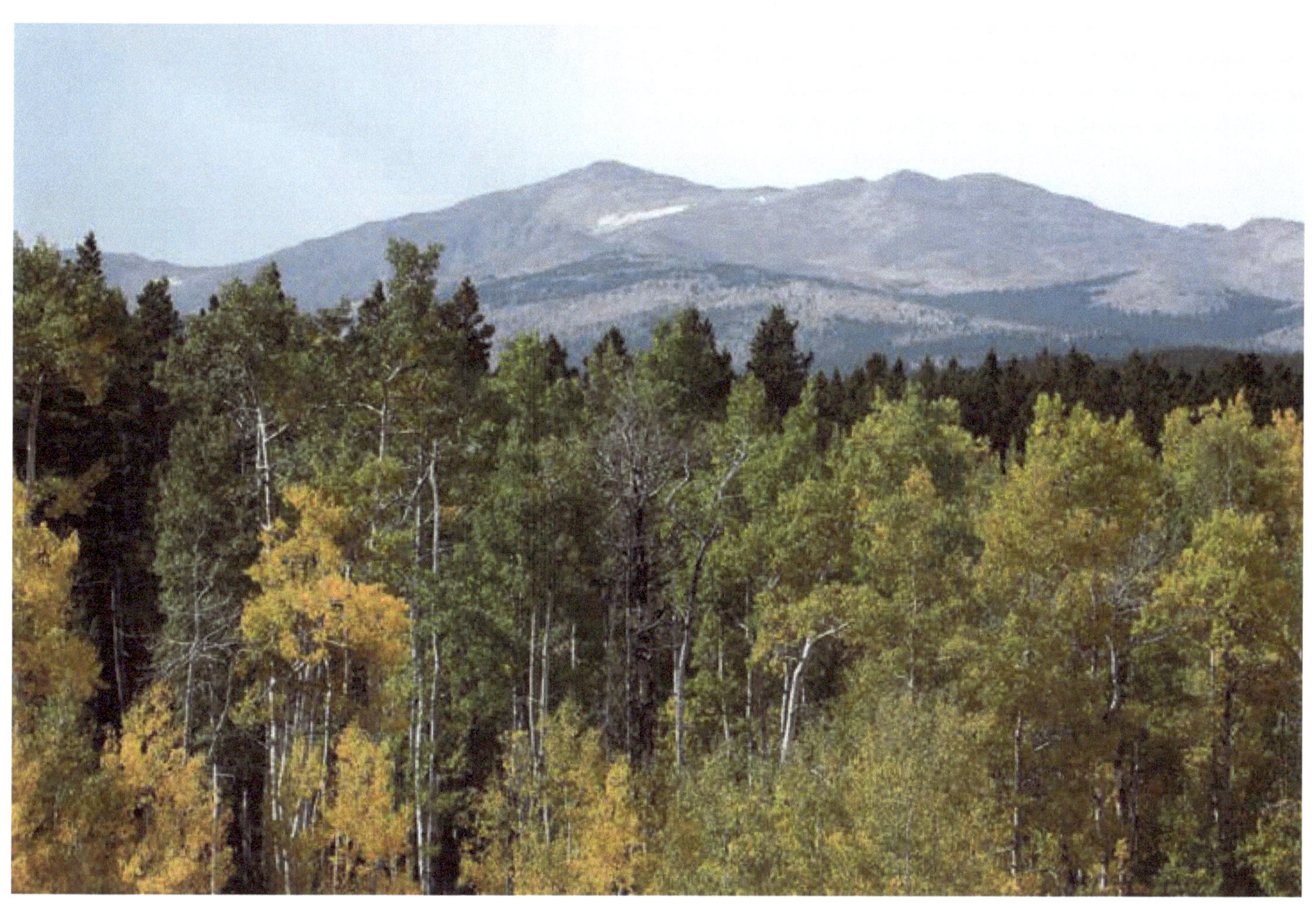

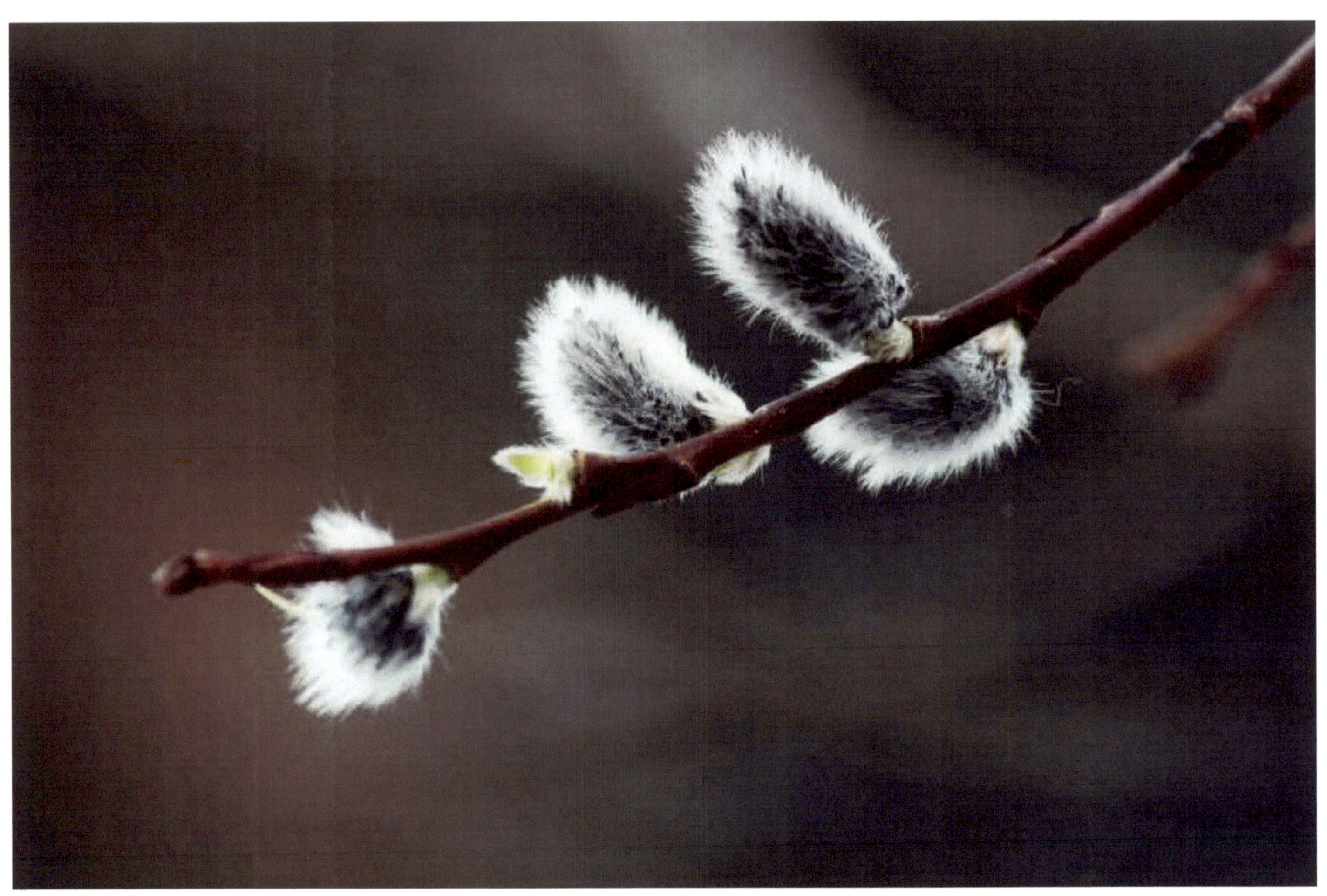

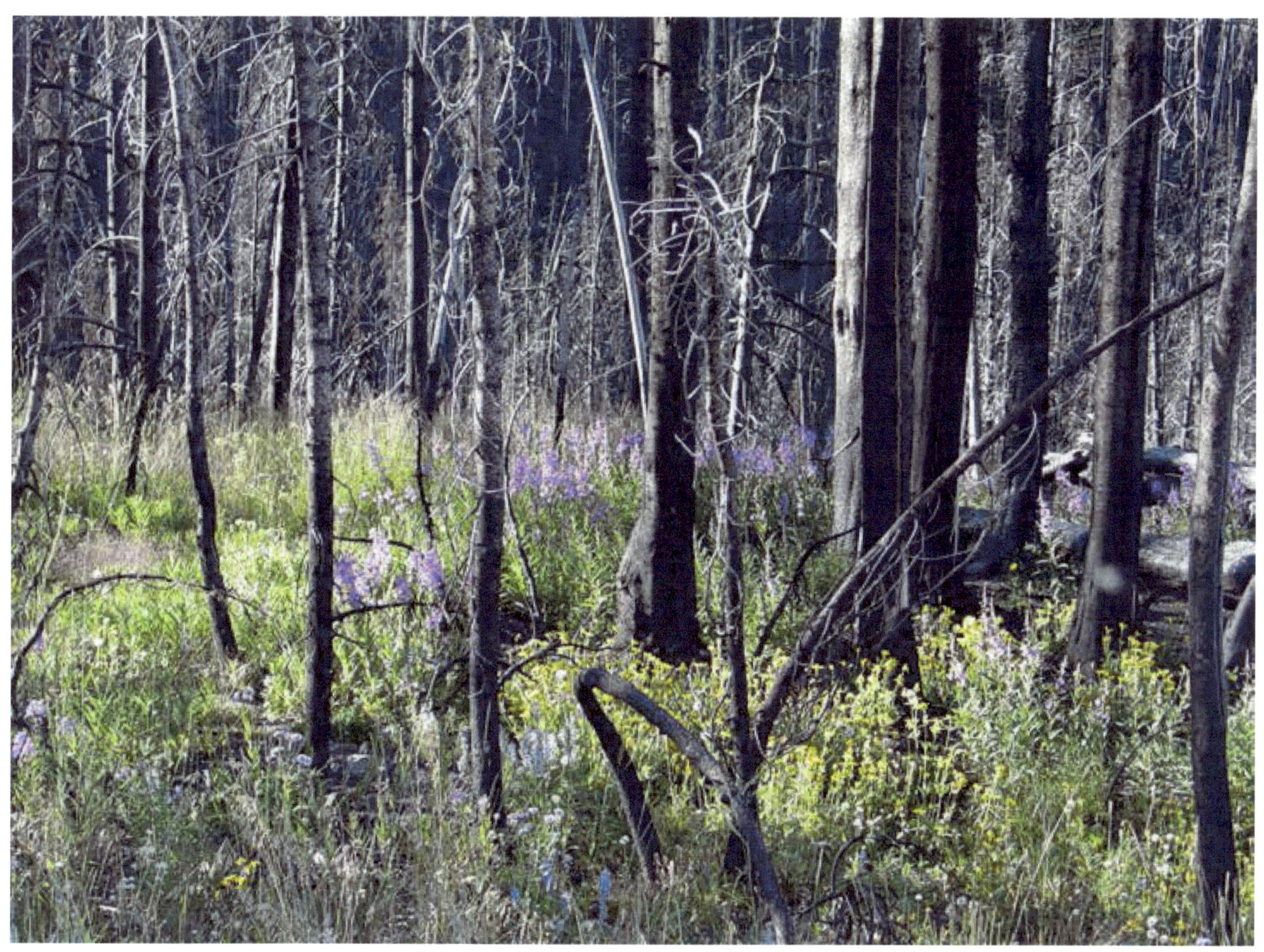

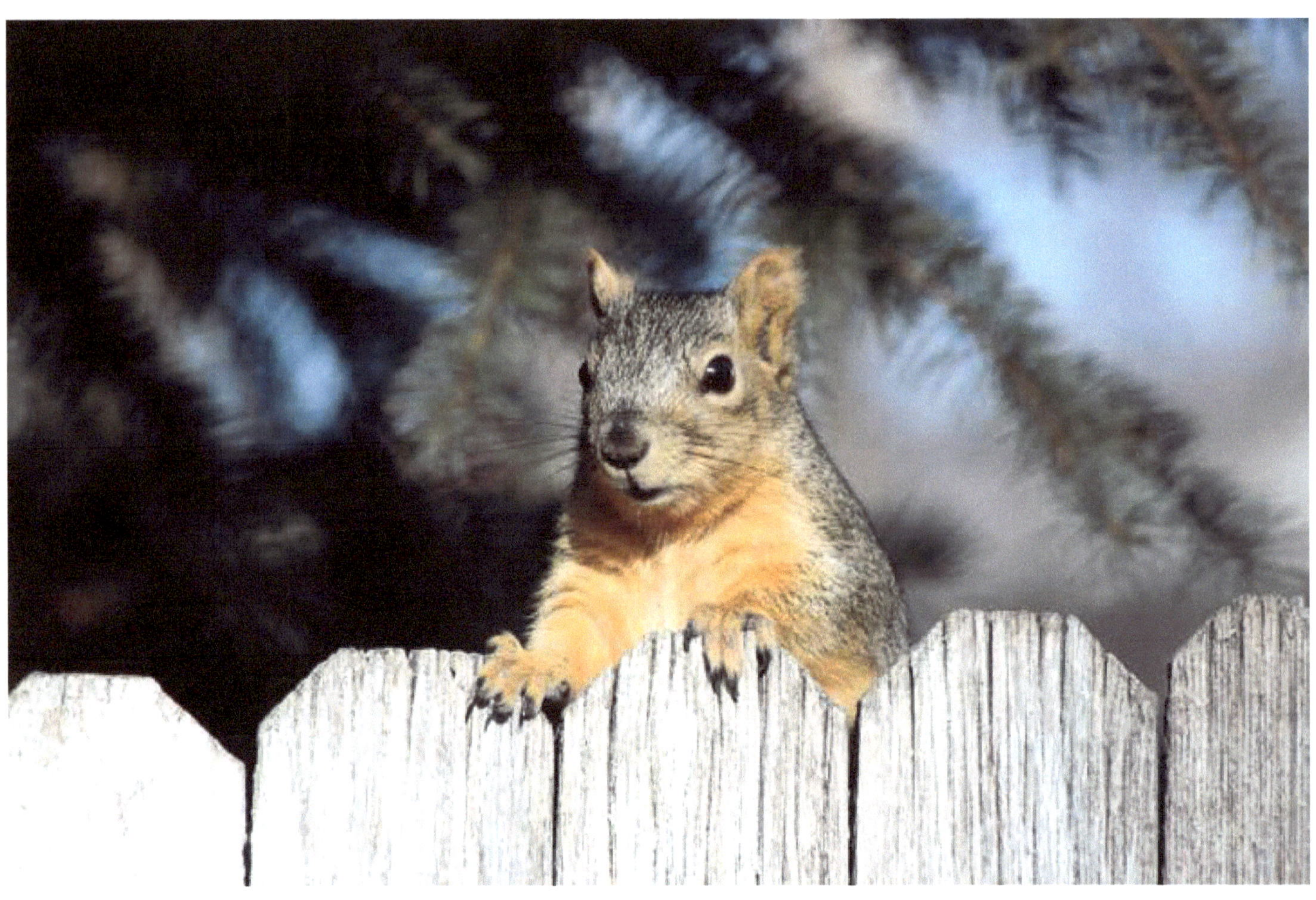

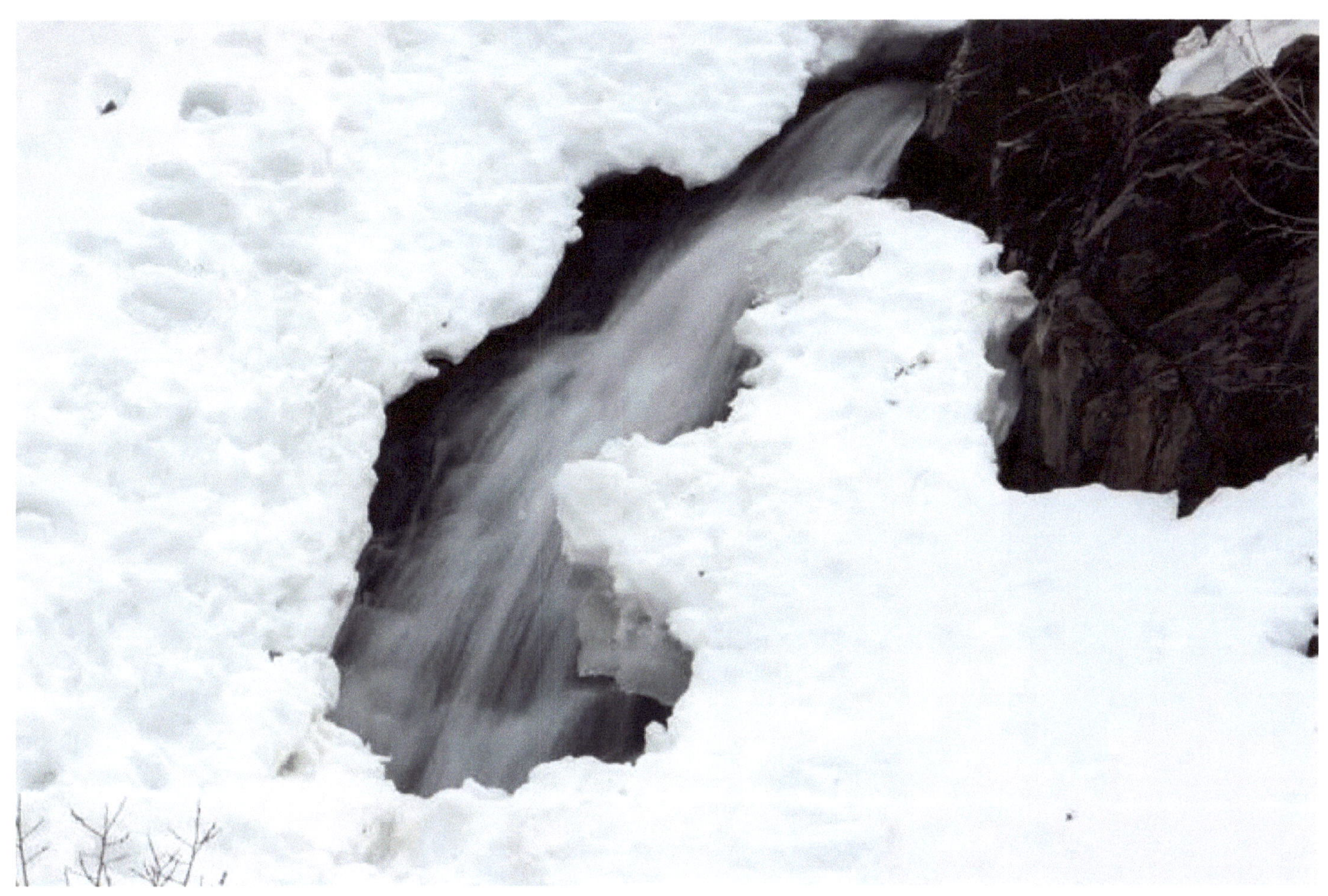

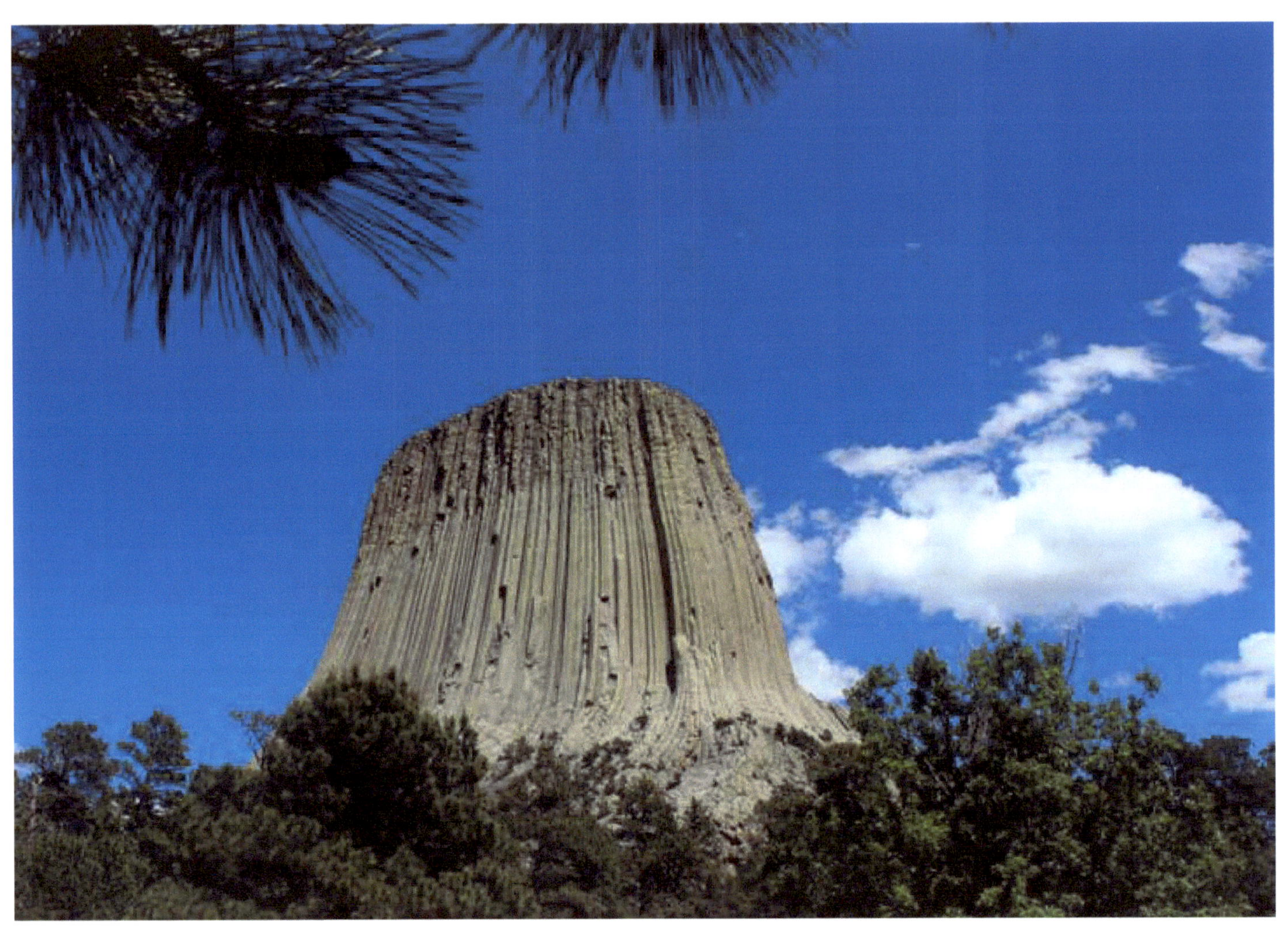

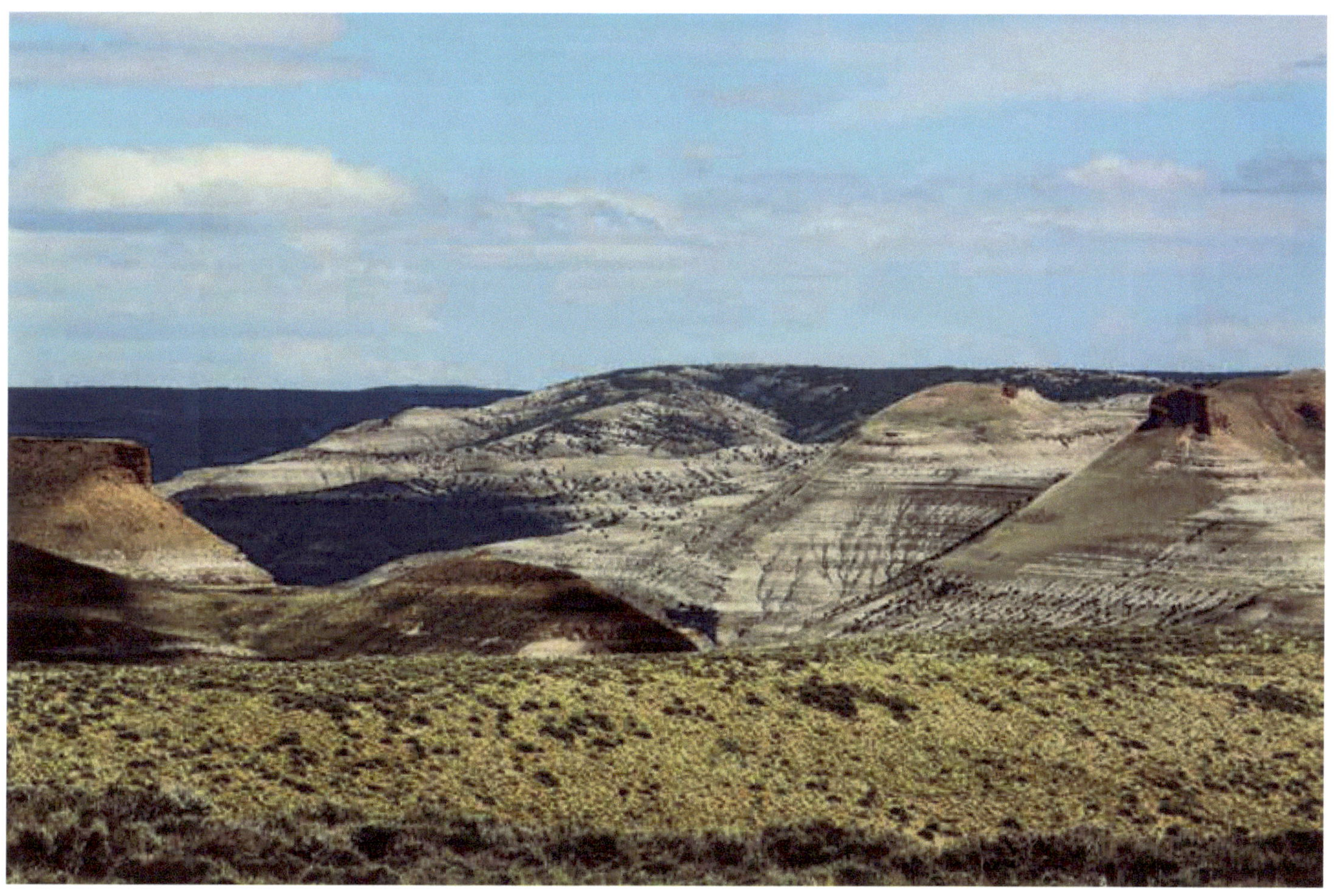

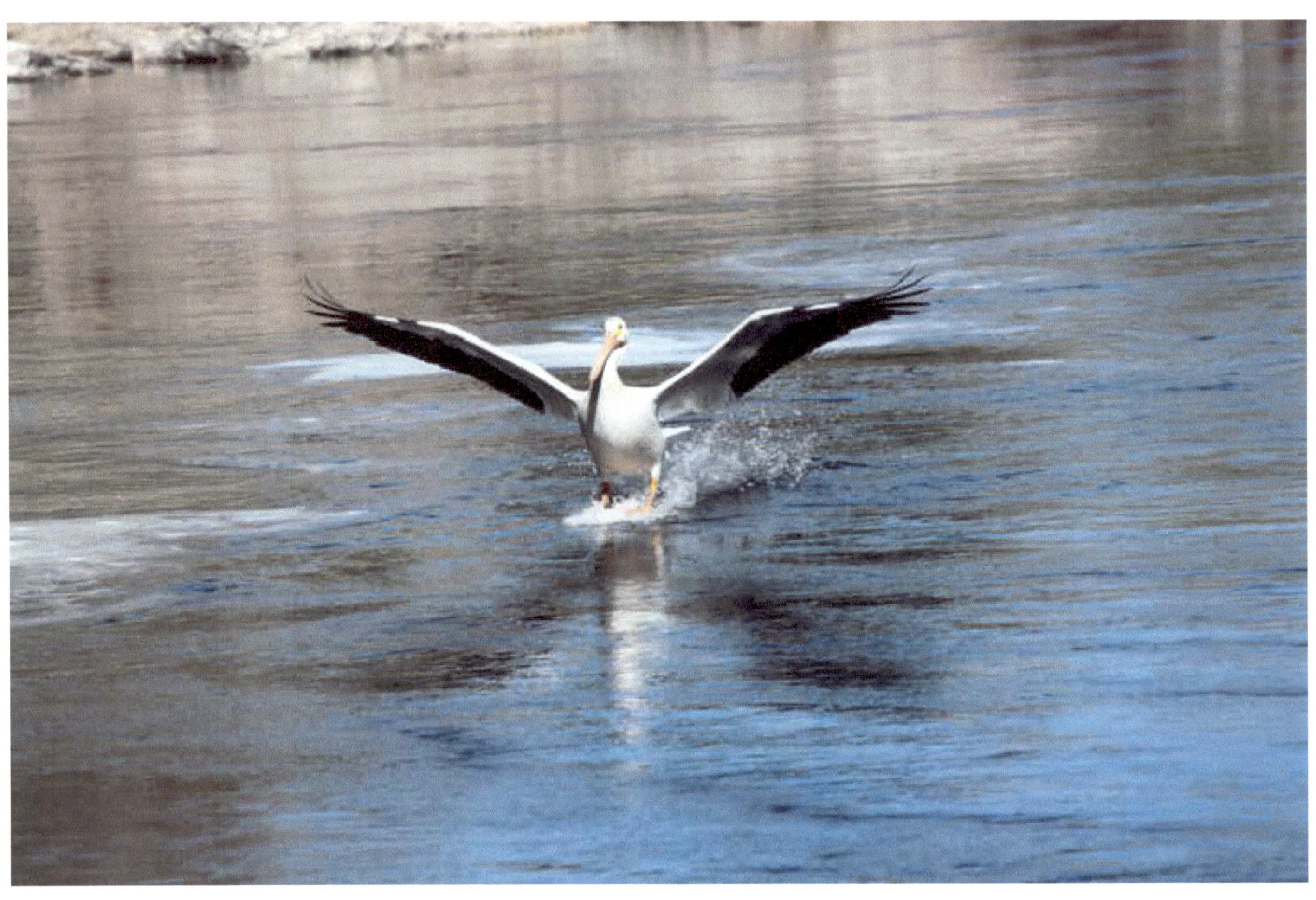

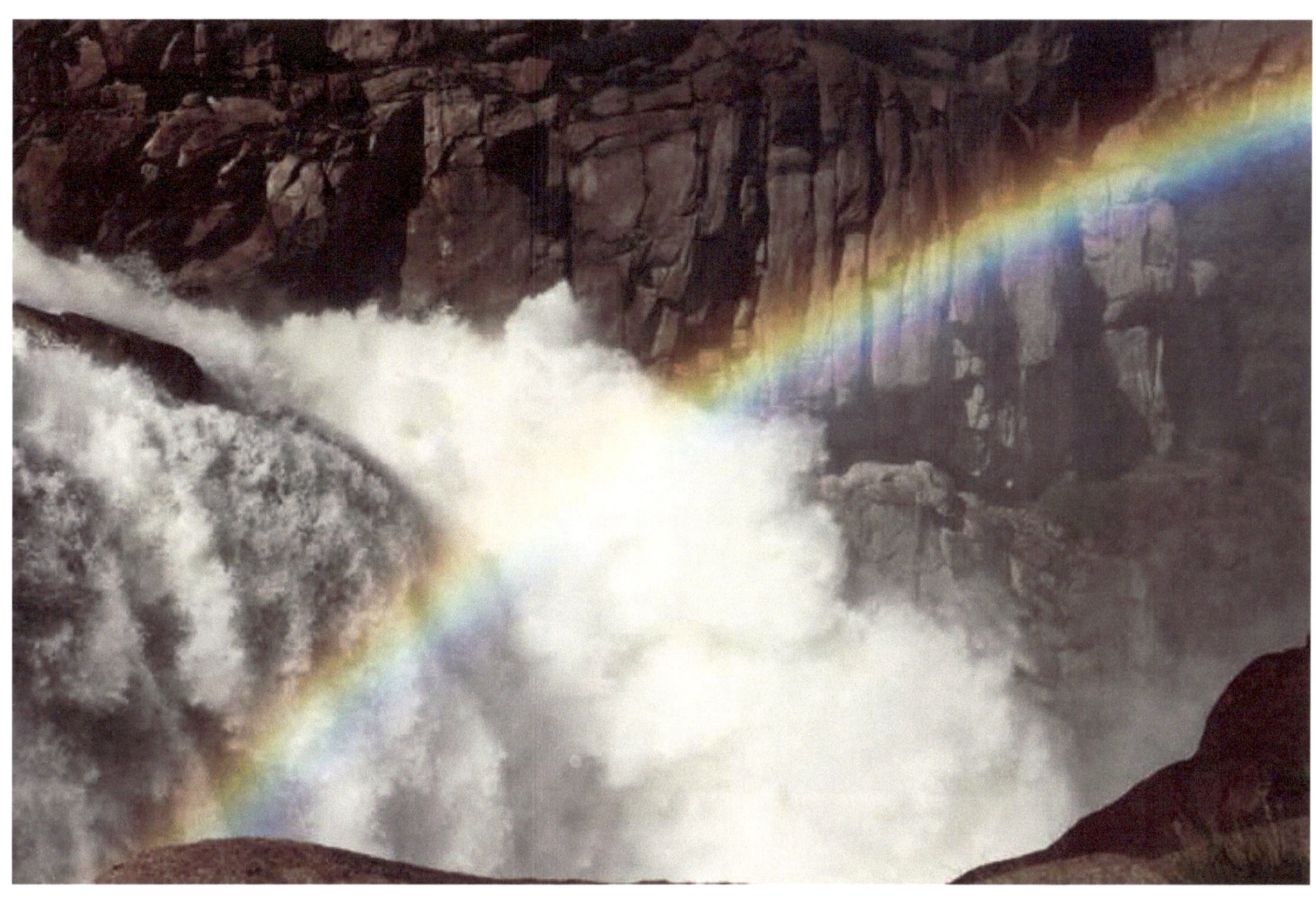

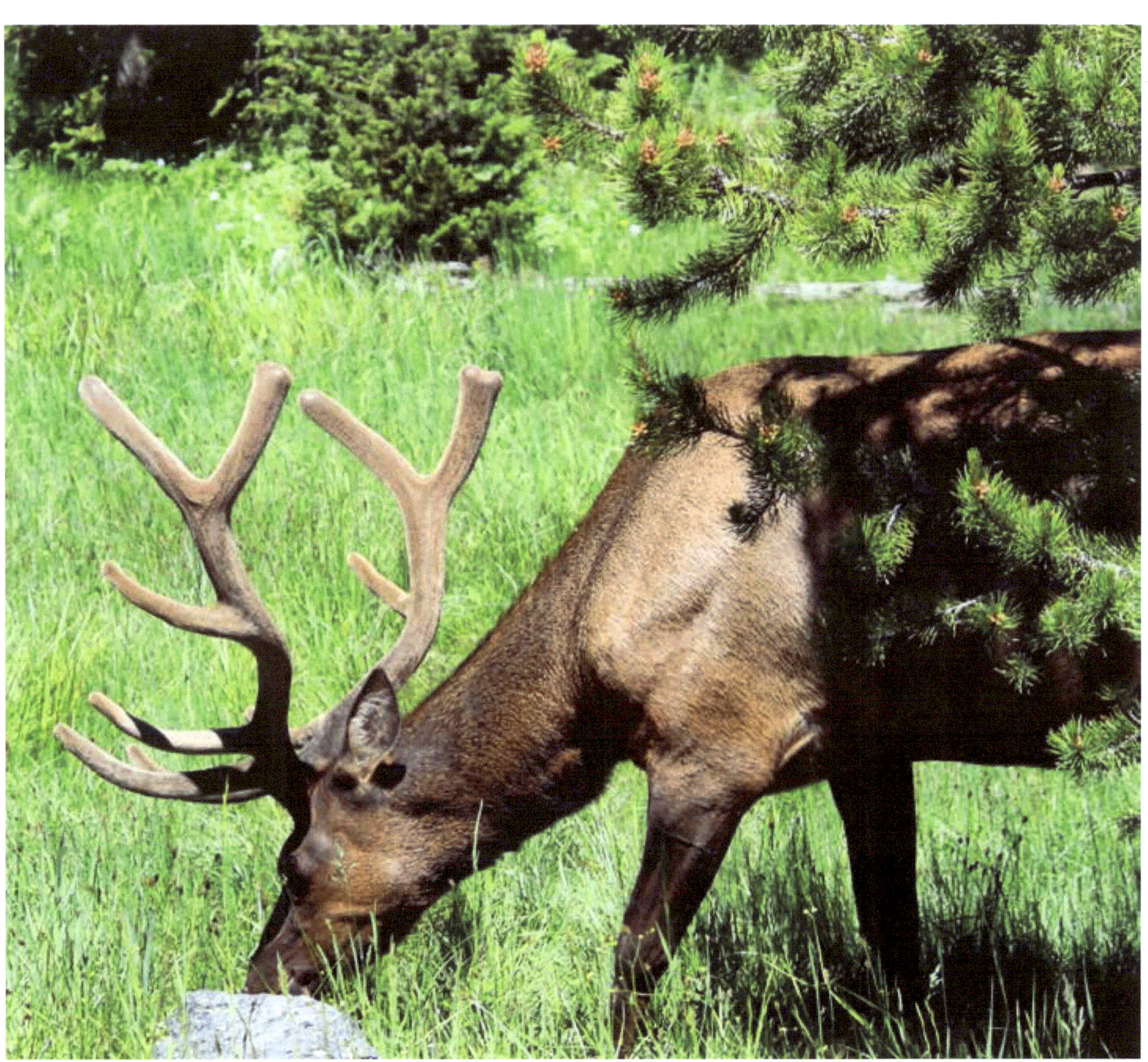

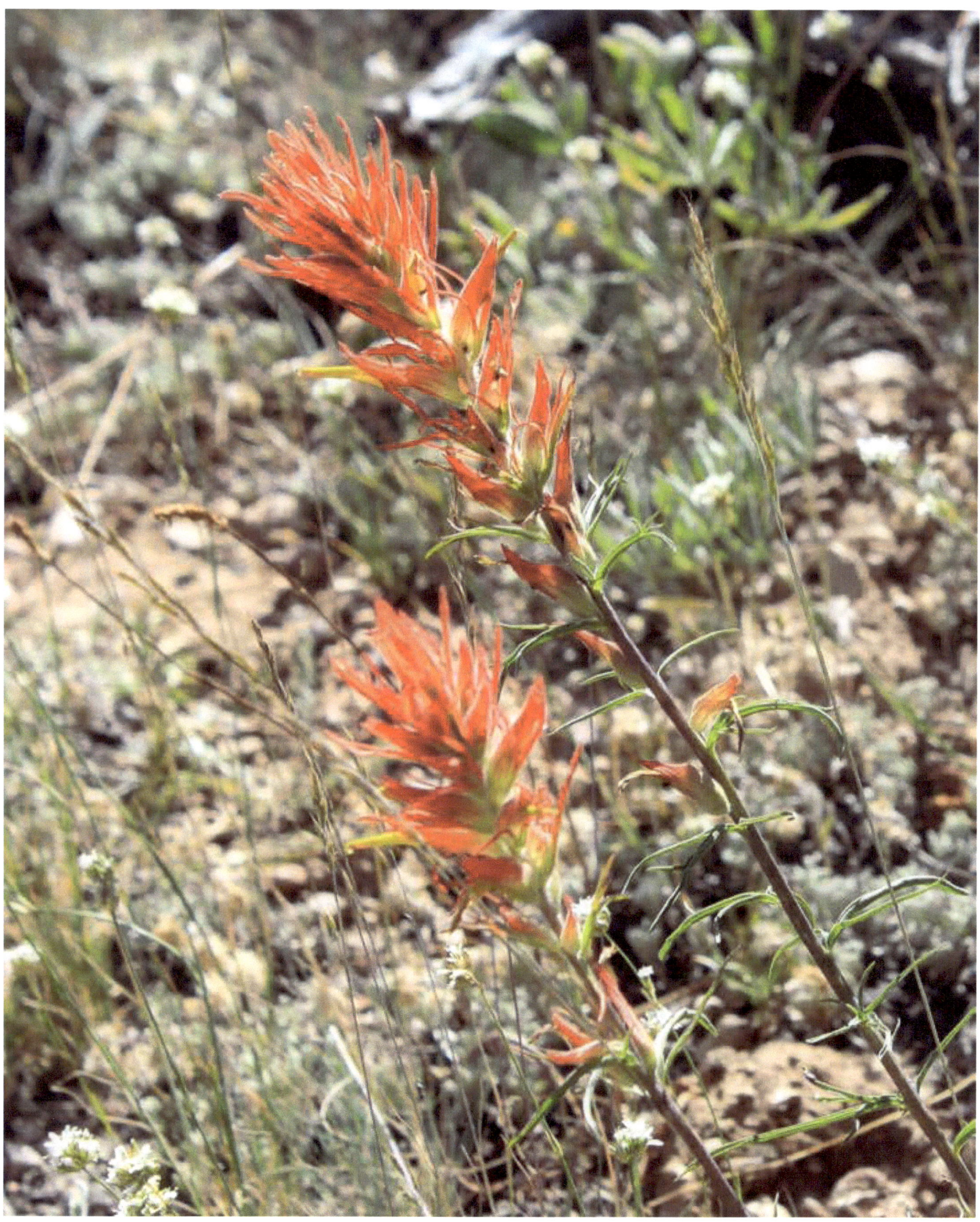

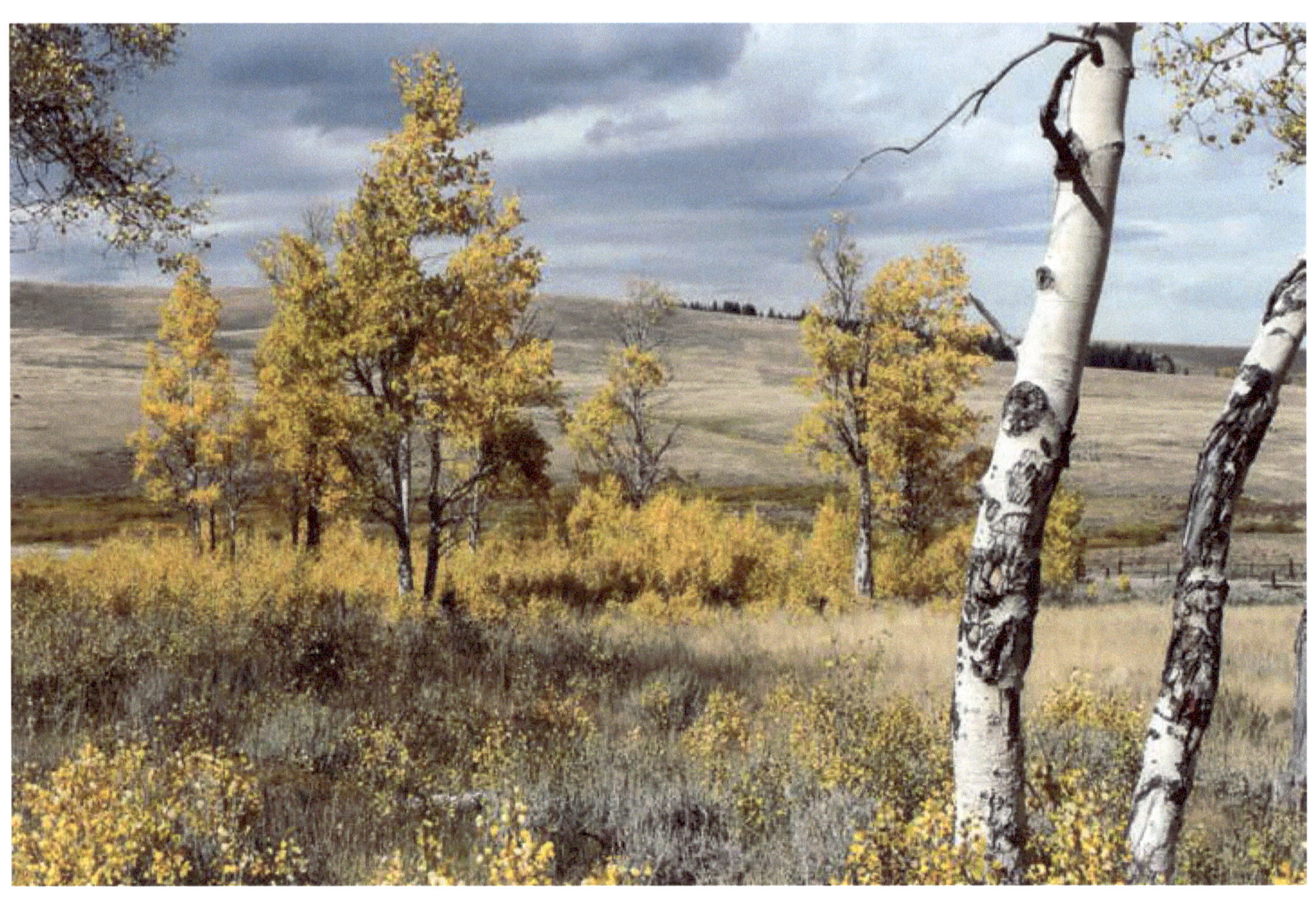

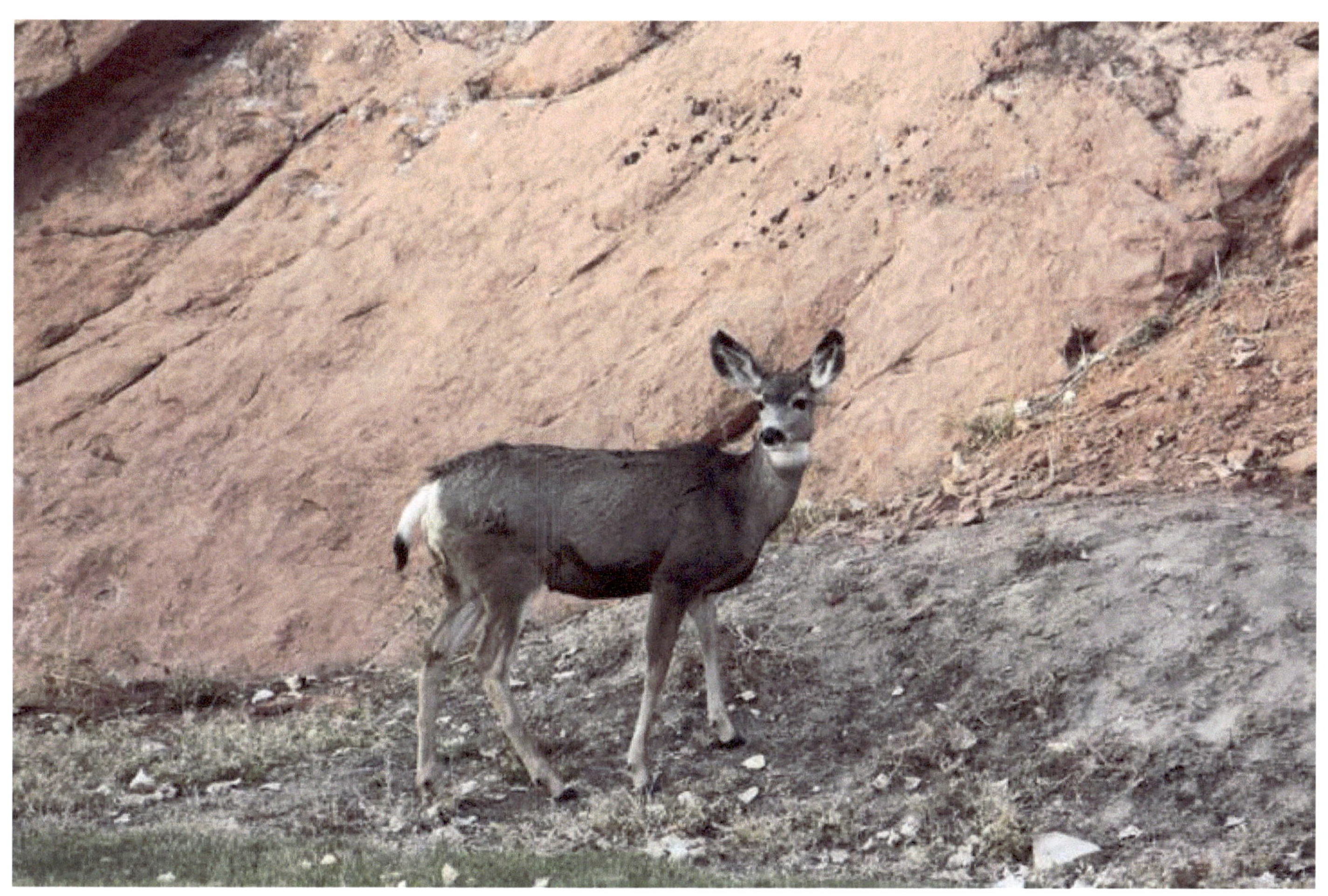

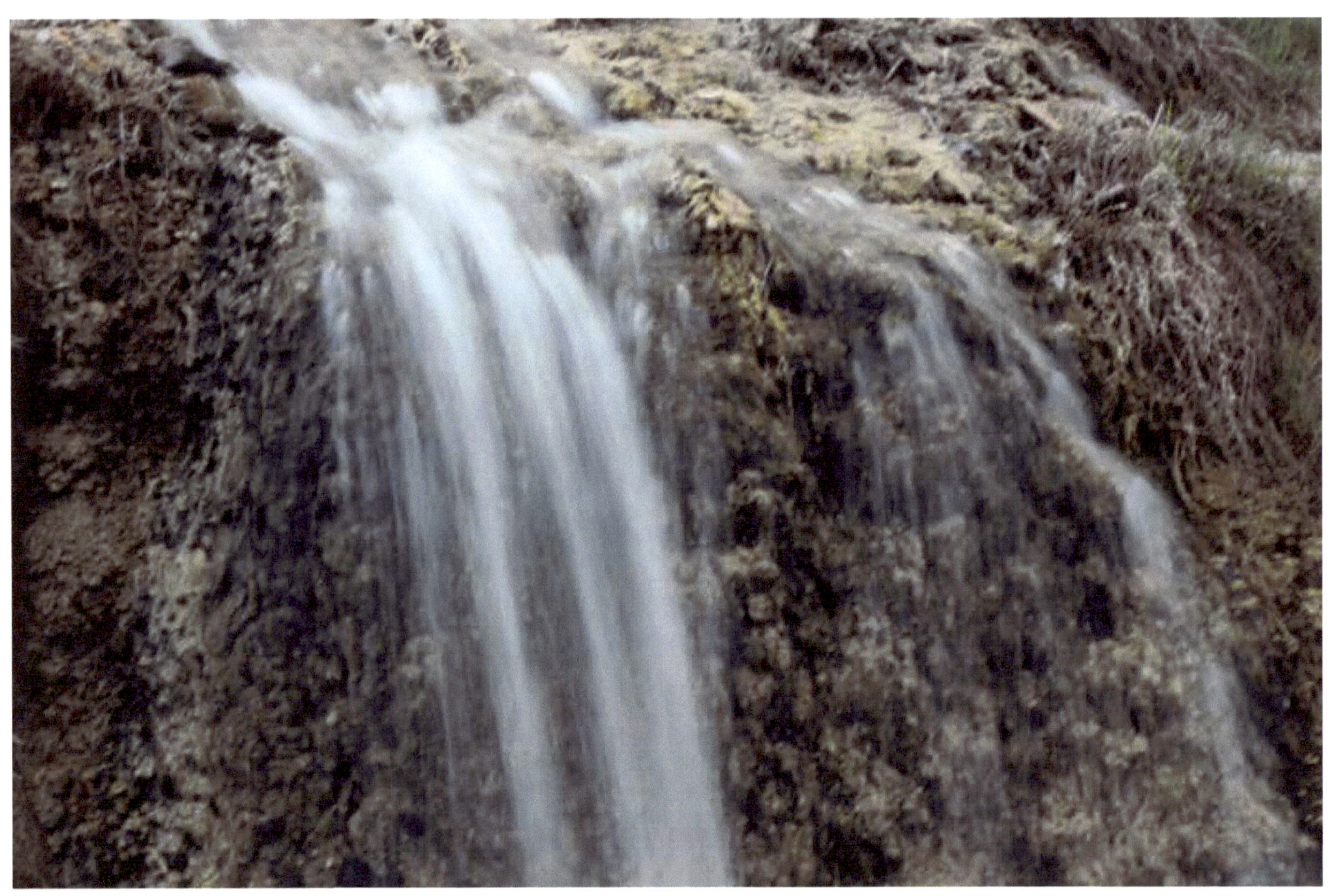

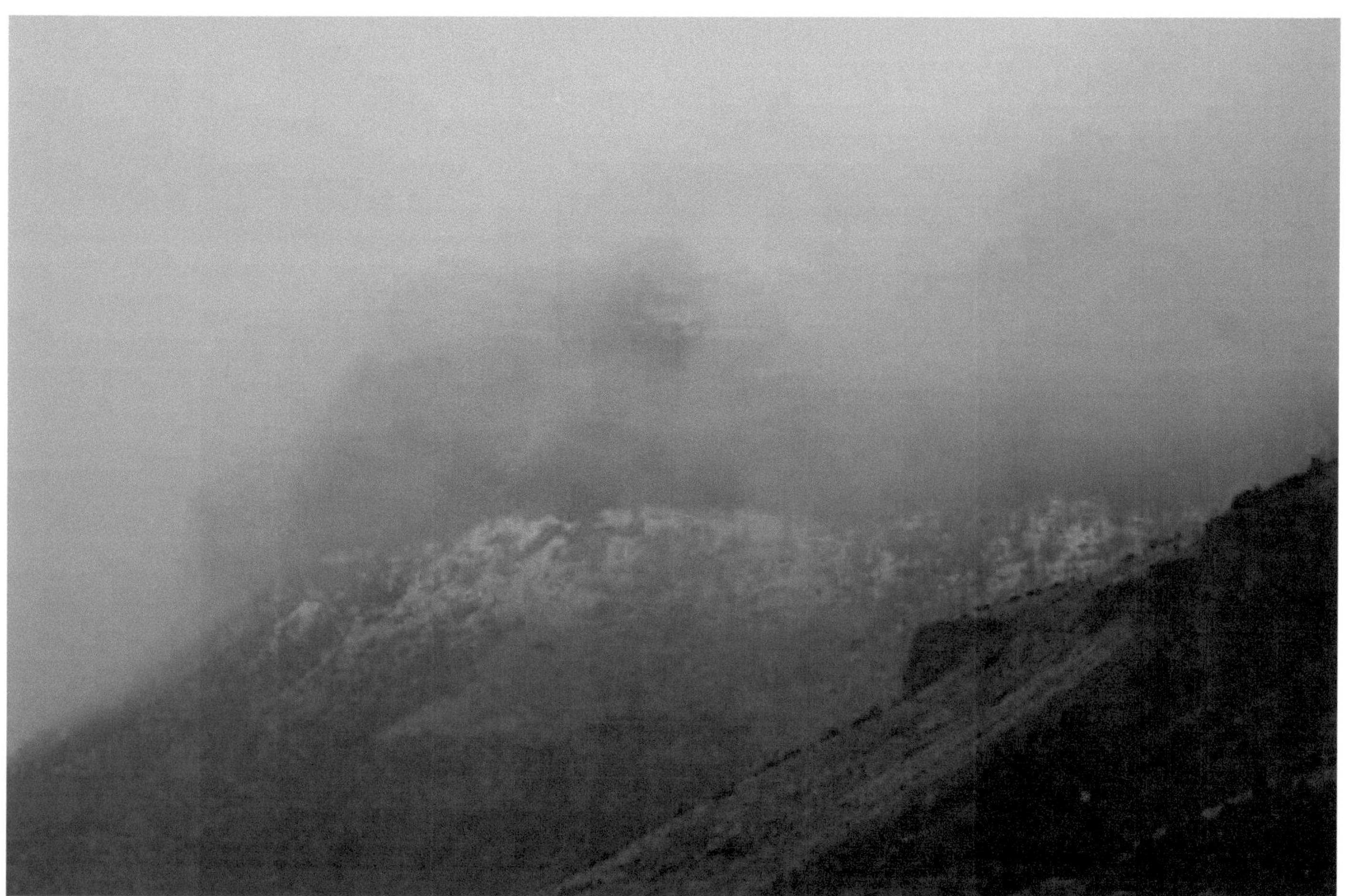

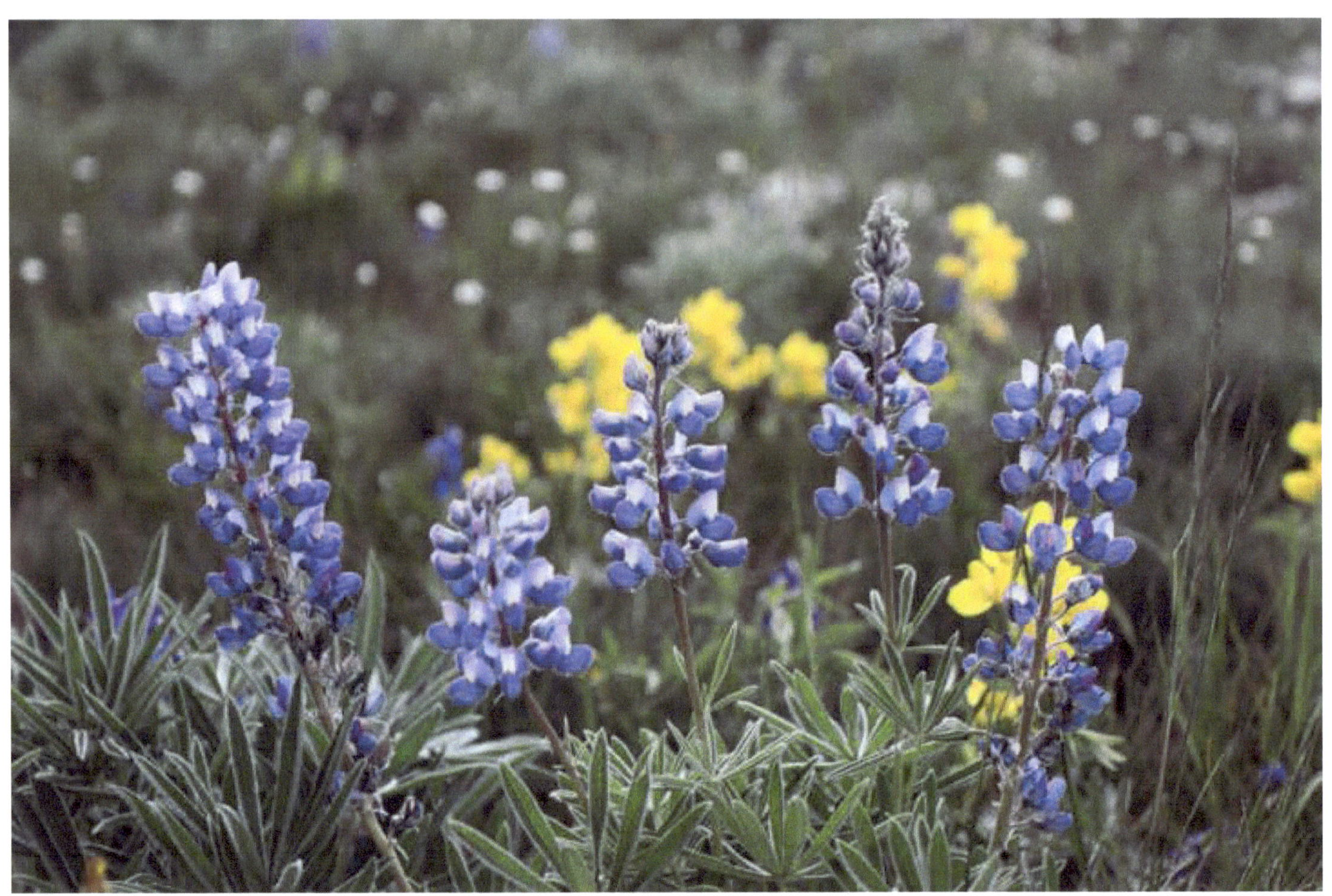

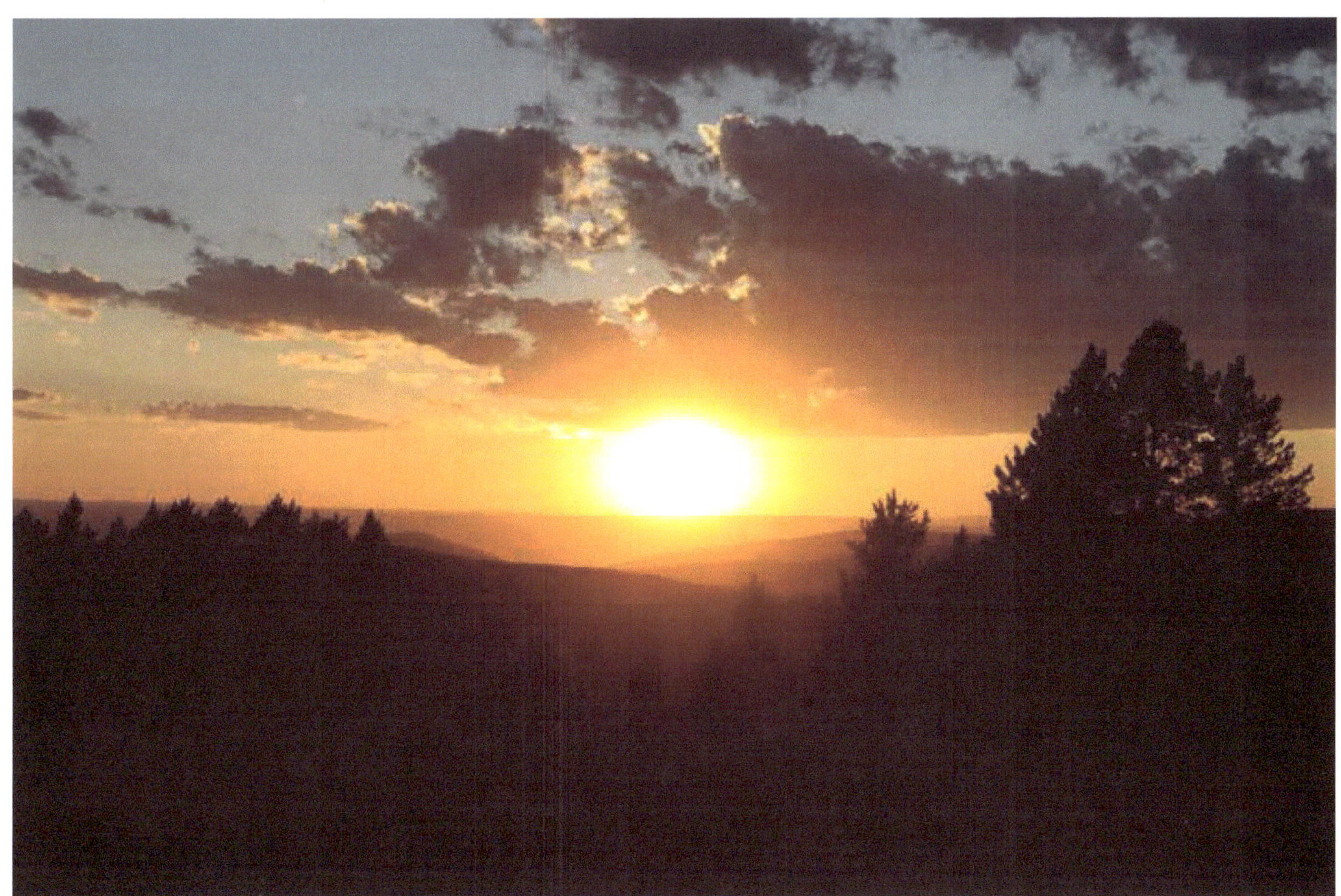

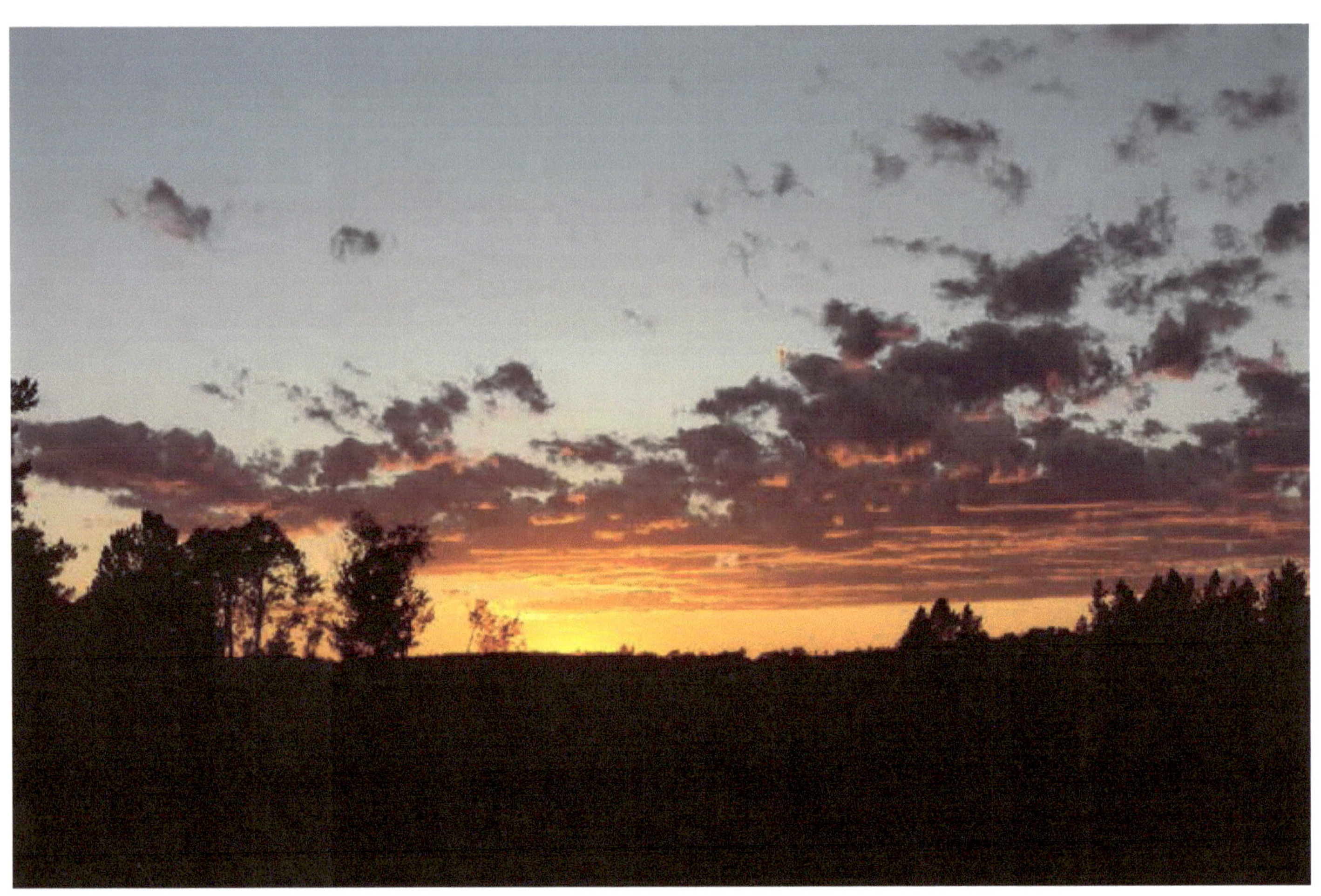

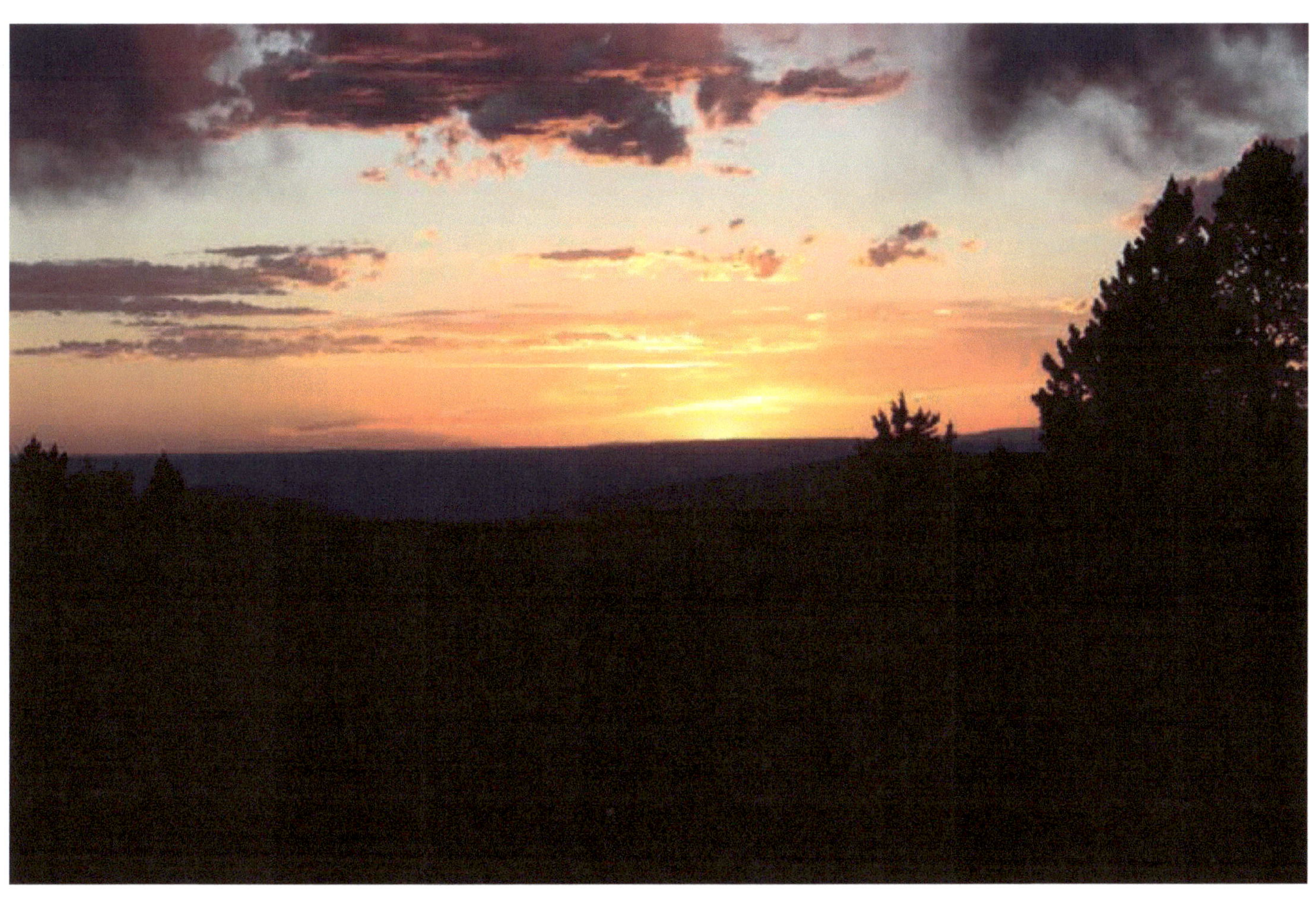